THIS JOURNAL BELONGS TO

____

www.ingramcontent.com/pod-product-compliance
Lightning Source LLC
Chambersburg PA
CBHW070603220526
45467CB00003B/1275
9781713167013